D0581791

You're Never Alone

*Words of encouragement
for those who have
lost a loved one*

*Written and compiled by
Elizabeth Rundle*

**kevin
mayhew**

First published in 2001 by
KEVIN MAYHEW LTD
Buxhall Stowmarket
Suffolk IP14 3BW

The publishers wish to express their gratitude to the following
for permission to include copyright material in this book:

Faber & Faber Ltd for the quote by C. S. Lewis (p. 9) taken from *A Grief Observed*.

Lion Publishing for the poem by Mary Hathaway (p. 15) from 'Why are you weeping?'

A. K. Weatherhead for the quote by Rev. D. Leslie Weatherhead (p. 17) from *A Private House of Prayers*.

The Leprosy Mission International for the quote by Eddie Askew (p. 19)
from *Facing the Storm*.

SPCK Publishing for the quote by David Adam (p. 21) from *Borderlands*.

Ronnie Barclay for the quote by William Barclay (p. 27).

Lakeland Publishers for the quote by John Jackson (p. 31)
from *It Was on a Monday Morning*.

Source Books for the poem by Edwina Gately (p. 31)
from 'Psalms of a laywoman'.

Scripture quotations are taken from *The Holy Bible, New International Version*
© 1973, 1978, 1984 International Bible Society. Used by permission of
Hodder & Stoughton Ltd. All rights reserved.

The publisher has made every effort to trace the owners of copyright
material and we hope that no copyright has been infringed. Pardon is sought
and apology made if the contrary be the case, and a correction will be made
in any reprint of this book.

9 8 7 6 5 4 3 2

ISBN 1 84003 753 9
Catalogue Number 1500436

Illustrations by Angela Palfrey
Cover design by Jonathan Stroulger
Edited and typeset by Elisabeth Bates
Printed and bound in China

An Appreciation

Bereavement is a curiously private experience. Perhaps this is because our friends and family do everything they can to help us cope. Most of us like to give the impression that we can manage the difficult things in life, so those who grieve often confide only in their diaries.

Elizabeth Rundle has done us all a service by allowing her own thoughts and feelings in the days, weeks and months after her husband's death to be published. The intensity of her emotions leaps from the page. A surge of unaccountable panic is a characteristic of bereavement, like a wave of tiredness upon waking to a new day. Gradually a calmer response emerges, and we see in these pages a growing sensitivity and compassion. It's a story of being refined by the grace which those who suffer seem often to be given. Even so, this collection of reflections on grief offers no easy application of the Christian hope, but the light of Christ is a constant glow in the background.

I can only imagine what it might be like to be widowed after years of marriage. I do know, however, what it is to be a bereaved parent, though strangely I'm not sure it makes me any better in my ministry to other parents who lose a child. Our human responses to similar experiences are varied, so we should not project our own feelings on to others. But we can speak of what we know. Elizabeth has done so for us of her own experience, and reading these pages has helped me interpret my own. I am grateful to her, and I am sure many others will be as well.

GRAHAM JAMES
BISHOP OF NORWICH

An Encouragement

Albert Schweitzer wrote about bereavement: 'Those who have learnt by experience . . . belong together all the world over; they are united by a secret bond.'

Grieving is such a painful process, and for each one of us it is an individual and unpredictable journey through darkness. My prayer is that some phrase or sentence from these pages may encourage others on their journey to hold on to the presence of God, and one day – the shadows will lift.

ELIZABETH RUNDLE

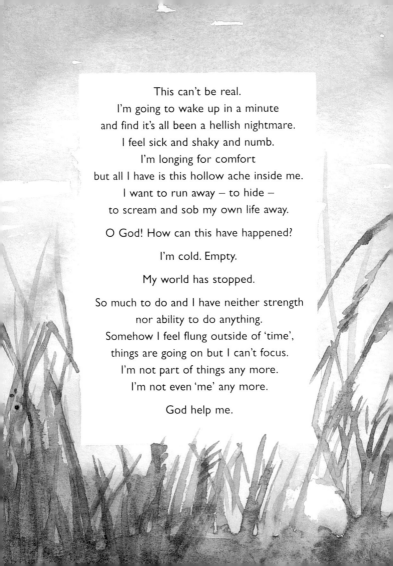

This can't be real.
I'm going to wake up in a minute
and find it's all been a hellish nightmare.
I feel sick and shaky and numb.
I'm longing for comfort
but all I have is this hollow ache inside me.
I want to run away – to hide –
to scream and sob my own life away.

O God! How can this have happened?

I'm cold. Empty.

My world has stopped.

So much to do and I have neither strength
nor ability to do anything.
Somehow I feel flung outside of 'time',
things are going on but I can't focus.
I'm not part of things any more.
I'm not even 'me' any more.

God help me.

O Lord, day and night I cry out . . .
I am confined and cannot escape;
my eyes are dim with grief.
Psalm 88:1, 8, 9

A voice is heard in Ramah,
mourning and great weeping,
Rachel weeping for her children
and refusing to be comforted
because her children are no more.
Jeremiah 31:15

Jesus said: 'Do not let your hearts be troubled.
Trust in God; trust also in me.'
John 14:1

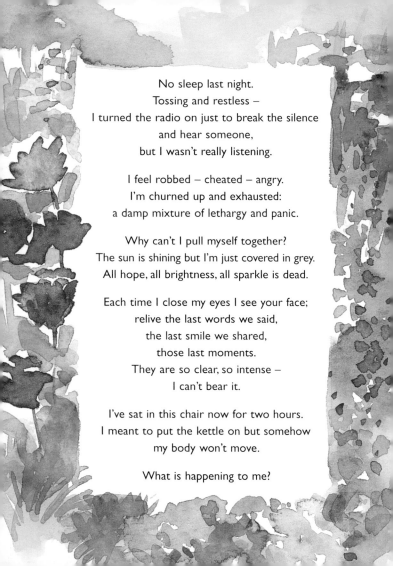

No sleep last night.
Tossing and restless –
I turned the radio on just to break the silence
and hear someone,
but I wasn't really listening.

I feel robbed – cheated – angry.
I'm churned up and exhausted:
a damp mixture of lethargy and panic.

Why can't I pull myself together?
The sun is shining but I'm just covered in grey.
All hope, all brightness, all sparkle is dead.

Each time I close my eyes I see your face;
relive the last words we said,
the last smile we shared,
those last moments.
They are so clear, so intense –
I can't bear it.

I've sat in this chair now for two hours.
I meant to put the kettle on but somehow
my body won't move.

What is happening to me?

*Save me, O God, for the waters
have come up to my neck.
I sink in the miry depths . . .
the floods engulf me. I am worn out.*
Psalm 69:1-3

*When Jesus saw Mary weeping he was
deeply moved in spirit and troubled . . .
Jesus wept.*
John 11: 33-35

*Jesus said:
'Blessed are those who mourn,
for they will be comforted.'*
Matthew 5:4

*No one ever told me that grief felt
so like fear. The same fluttering in
the stomach, the same restlessness,
the yawning. I keep on swallowing.*
C. S. Lewis

I'm afraid of the future.
Will I cope?

Do other people feel like this?
Raw – ripped open.
I keep crying.

People mean well –
but they just don't understand.
No one knows what is going on inside my mind.

I feel so alone.
Maybe if I concentrate on happy memories,
if I focus clearly enough,
then I may feel you here again.

How long must I wrestle with my thoughts
and every day have sorrow in my heart?
Psalm 13

'*My God, my God,*
why have you forsaken me?'
Psalm 22

For those who are suffering
the agony of bereavement,
who cry out from their hearts,
and, perhaps for a time
find it hard to pray and to hold on to God,
the secret lies here:
We do not have to hold on to God –
He will hold us until such time
as we are feeling stronger again.
Frazer D. Smith

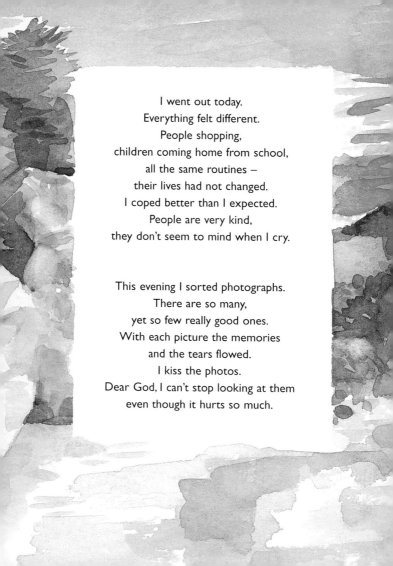

I went out today.
Everything felt different.
People shopping,
children coming home from school,
all the same routines –
their lives had not changed.
I coped better than I expected.
People are very kind,
they don't seem to mind when I cry.

This evening I sorted photographs.
There are so many,
yet so few really good ones.
With each picture the memories
and the tears flowed.
I kiss the photos.
Dear God, I can't stop looking at them
even though it hurts so much.

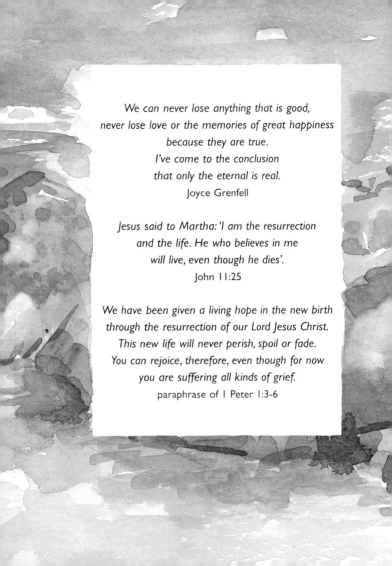

We can never lose anything that is good,
never lose love or the memories of great happiness
because they are true.
I've come to the conclusion
that only the eternal is real.
Joyce Grenfell

Jesus said to Martha: 'I am the resurrection
and the life. He who believes in me
will live, even though he dies'.
John 11:25

We have been given a living hope in the new birth
through the resurrection of our Lord Jesus Christ.
This new life will never perish, spoil or fade.
You can rejoice, therefore, even though for now
you are suffering all kinds of grief.
paraphrase of 1 Peter 1:3-6

Friends are such a comfort.
Instead of just blaming God,
I can thank him for giving me
these 'guardian angels'.

I long to hear words of hope and faith –
words from someone who understands –
words that will give me peace.
All the New Testament writers were
so positive that Jesus rose up from the dead.

I'm desperate to be positive.

Death has always been
someone else's problem.
I've been sad for them,
sent many sympathy cards,
I was sincere but I didn't understand.

I am so tired.

Perhaps death is something like
leaving the womb.
From a known existence in fluid,
to a new experience of light and air.
Please God there will be loving hands
of welcome and joy,
and the other side of death,
the new life.

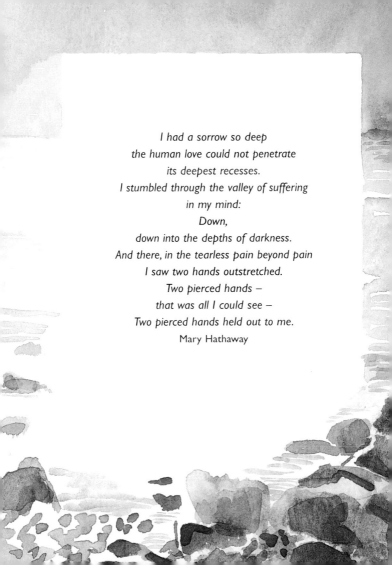

I had a sorrow so deep
the human love could not penetrate
its deepest recesses.
I stumbled through the valley of suffering
in my mind:
Down,
down into the depths of darkness.
And there, in the tearless pain beyond pain
I saw two hands outstretched.
Two pierced hands –
that was all I could see –
Two pierced hands held out to me.

Mary Hathaway

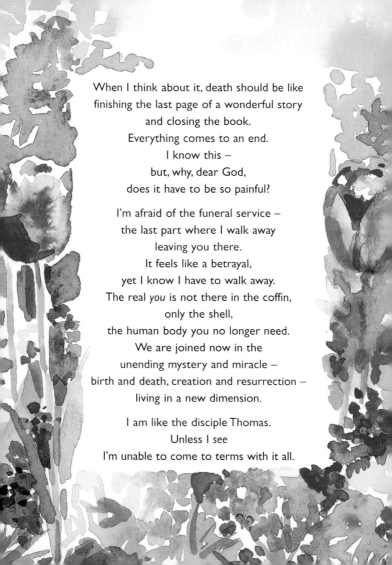

When I think about it, death should be like
finishing the last page of a wonderful story
and closing the book.
Everything comes to an end.
I know this –
but, why, dear God,
does it have to be so painful?

I'm afraid of the funeral service –
the last part where I walk away
leaving you there.
It feels like a betrayal,
yet I know I have to walk away.
The real *you* is not there in the coffin,
only the shell,
the human body you no longer need.
We are joined now in the
unending mystery and miracle –
birth and death, creation and resurrection –
living in a new dimension.

I am like the disciple Thomas.
Unless I *see*
I'm unable to come to terms with it all.

We give them back to you, O God,
for you gave them to us,
and as you did not lose them in the giving,
so we believe we cannot lose them in their return.
For Life is Eternal, and Love is Immortal,
and death is only a horizon,
a horizon being just the limit
of our human sight.
So lift us up, O God,
that we may feel nearer our loved one
who is with you.
adapted from a prayer by Bishop Brent

More and more we must come to see death
in a new way. Think of it not as a calamity
but as a milestone; not an end
but a beginning to a wonderful experience
much more worth calling 'Life' than
anything we have yet imagined.
D. Leslie Weatherhead

The Lord is here: his Spirit is with us.

The funeral is today. I'm dreading it.

It all seems so final.
Up till now I've been living and talking in the past –
almost pretending it hasn't really happened.

I don't see you any more.
Where are you?
Are you going through the hell of parting like me?

God, help me through this.

The souls of the just are in God's hands
and torment shall not touch them.
In the eyes of foolish men they seem to be dead:
their departure reckoned as defeat
and their going from us as disaster.
But they are at peace.
Wisdom of Solomon 3:1-3

However dark the road, however long it takes,
there comes a point where we break through our
personal pain barrier onto a smoother road ahead.
The real miracle is not that something spectacular
has happened, but that we found the courage
and strength to keep going. Then we can look back
and find the Lord was with us.
Eddie Askew

Jesus promised: 'I am with you always . . .'
Matthew 28: 20

For God so loved the world that he gave his only Son
that whosoever believes in him should not perish
but have eternal life.
John 3:16

The funeral is over now.
Everyone has gone.
Yes, it was comforting in a way.
It felt right but it all went so quickly.
So now I have to readjust –
to rebuild my life –
make a new routine.

Everything is so different.

But God is the same.
Love is the same.
My family and my friends are the same.
Outwardly, I suppose, I am the same.
Dear God, help me to build on all the goodness
from 'before'.
Show me how to focus on new priorities.
Just give me the strength
to drag myself into tomorrow.

*Faith is putting your hand out in the dark
and finding it held.*

*Let the morning bring me word of your
unfailing love,
for I have put my trust in you.
Show me the way I should go . . .*
Psalm 143:8

*We are not self-sufficient, even though we like to
give the appearance that we are. We learn that
we need help from outside, from a power that
is greater than our power.*
David Adam

*In gratitude and love, I will say in my hours of fear
and distress: 'My Father, I do not understand but
I trust thee'.*
A plaque on one of the ancient olive trees
in the garden of Gethsemane

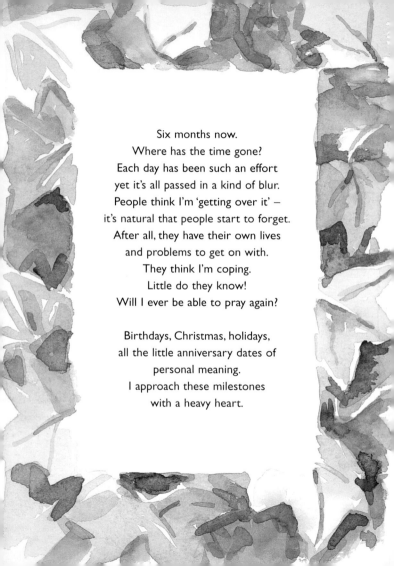

Six months now.
Where has the time gone?
Each day has been such an effort
yet it's all passed in a kind of blur.
People think I'm 'getting over it' –
it's natural that people start to forget.
After all, they have their own lives
and problems to get on with.
They think I'm coping.
Little do they know!
Will I ever be able to pray again?

Birthdays, Christmas, holidays,
all the little anniversary dates of
personal meaning.
I approach these milestones
with a heavy heart.

Don't be afraid to pray –
to pray is sometimes the only thing we can do.
Keep going . . . keep praying.
Pray through the shadow and the darkness,
pray through the Gethsemane experience.
God is there.
J. S. Steward

Sometimes I can laugh – then I feel guilty,
then laughter comes perilously close to tears.
Surely, the worst is behind me now.
Thank you, Lord,
for the people who have stayed by me –
they have been my life-line.

Self-pity is a dangerous indulgence!
It can set a course for self-destruction.
Am I honestly ready to wither?
To give up?
There is an alternative –
Lord, help me
to pick up the threads of my life again.

Lord, you are like a weaver in our lives –
you have spun each one of us into a unique
and colourful strand . . .
then you wove us together.

Lord, Great Weaver,
open our eyes to the mystery and
power of your Spirit.

Reattach us to your loom
through the power of Christ.
Together in Prayer:
Women's World Day of Prayer, 1993

I've discovered 'prayer' again.
Not in so many words
but coming to God in my blankness,
waiting to receive
rather than struggle for the right things to say.
This kind of praying is new to me
but it doesn't matter.
I must hang on to the shreds of my faith,
keep going through the crucifying experience –
God is there.
God is with me.
I am not alone.

There was a weed pushing up through the pavement.
What a life-force in that tiny green shoot.
Against all odds it pushed upwards
and found the light.
I've got to be like that, Lord.
If a wisp of a weed can do it – I can.
I will, God being my helper.

We know that death is not the end
but the beginning of Life.
We know ourselves not to be
the children of a moment,
but pilgrims of eternity.
William Barclay

God himself will be with them and be their God.
He will wipe every tear from their eyes.
There will be no more death or mourning
or crying or pain,
for the old order of things has passed away . . .
Behold – I make all things new.
Revelation 21:3-5

Things have been easier lately.
I've forgotten myself at times – I feel better.
Better physically, emotionally and spiritually.
Thank you, Lord.

Looking back I do believe
that I have been guided.
There are feelings of gratitude now
rather than nagging resentment and bitterness.
I have been given inner strength –
and yes, even inner peace.
Perhaps I'm not raging and fighting any more.

It was never so obvious before
how everything is constantly on the change.
The changing seasons
with changing weather and colours,
children growing up, friends moving away,
shops changing hands, new estates being built,
all change, swept along
by natural rhythm and movement –
me too.

I wonder what 'heaven' is like.

Someone will ask:'How are the dead raised?
With what kind of body do they come?' Fool!
What you sow does not come to life unless it dies.
And as for what you sow, you do not sow
the body that is to be . . .
But God gives it a body as he has chosen,
and to each kind of seed its own body . . .
So it is with the resurrection of the dead . . .
It is sown a physical body,
it is raised a spiritual body.
1 Corinthians 15:35-44

What is seen is temporary,
but what is unseen is eternal.
2 Corinthians 4:18

Up and down today.
A bit of a wobbly day.
Wallowing is an unproductive pastime.

Thank you, Lord,
for the memories which bring smiles –
we never appreciate just how sweet they are
until they become irreplaceable.
I cling to the memories with warmest love.

Lord, help me to be positive.
Just a small step forward each day.

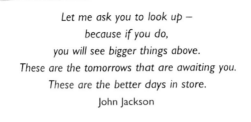

Let me ask you to look up –
because if you do,
you will see bigger things above.
These are the tomorrows that are awaiting you.
These are the better days in store.

John Jackson

Into your hands, Lord,
this solitude;
into your hands, Lord,
this emptiness;
into your hands, Lord,
this loneliness;
into your hands, Lord,
this grief;
into your hands, Lord,
what is left of me.

Edwina Gately

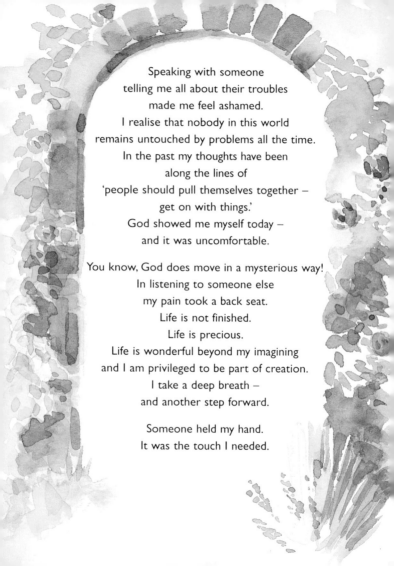

Speaking with someone
telling me all about their troubles
made me feel ashamed.
I realise that nobody in this world
remains untouched by problems all the time.
In the past my thoughts have been
along the lines of
'people should pull themselves together –
get on with things.'
God showed me myself today –
and it was uncomfortable.

You know, God does move in a mysterious way!
In listening to someone else
my pain took a back seat.
Life is not finished.
Life is precious.
Life is wonderful beyond my imagining
and I am privileged to be part of creation.
I take a deep breath –
and another step forward.

Someone held my hand.
It was the touch I needed.

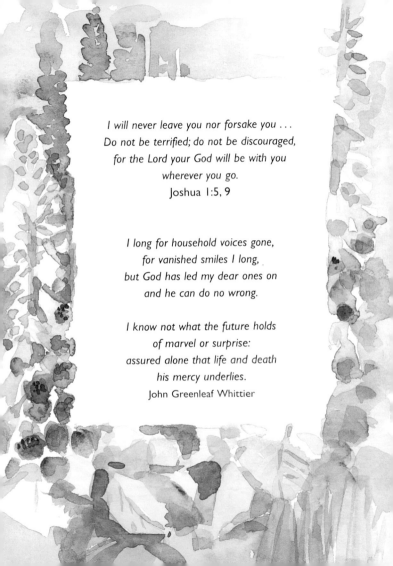

I will never leave you nor forsake you . . .
Do not be terrified; do not be discouraged,
for the Lord your God will be with you
wherever you go.
Joshua 1:5, 9

I long for household voices gone,
for vanished smiles I long,
but God has led my dear ones on
and he can do no wrong.

I know not what the future holds
of marvel or surprise:
assured alone that life and death
his mercy underlies.
John Greenleaf Whittier

No use pretending Light banishes
the Gloom at a stroke.
The whole process of grieving
is slow and irrational,
inconclusive and disorientating.
The brittle bonds of bereavement
are like a casing from which I can only emerge
when I am ready.
But there is fear in the breaking out –
too many tender emotions.

I am surprised by the 'me' who is emerging.
Not exactly a new 'me',
but definitely a kinder, more tolerant human being.
Abrasive edges have softened now.
I understand compassion.

Mystery and Miracle have been washed by
the tears of experience and through these
sometimes raging storms, my resurrection
faith has become absolute.

It is our inner security that enables us
to cope with the outer insecurities.
Betty Hares

Christian people believe in the strong love of God ...
that love does not answer all questions,
nor does it protect us from the bad times.
But from experience, ours, and others,
we perhaps begin to learn that it is strong
and it will see us through.
N. Collinson and D. Matthews

I know that my Redeemer lives!
Job 19:25

Time marches on.
Relentlessly . . . time disappears –
it is nearly a year now,
a whole year!
Times remembered but so much forgotten.
I am able to speak with fond laughter now,
and remembering brings a comforting peace.
I need to talk and I need to remember.

Tears may still fall at times,
but they are not so blinding,
not so paralysing in their intensity.

Healing is a long process.
There is no steady upward path,
rather the unpredictable ups and downs
of day by day, night by night,
then, gradually, composure is regained,
confidence creeps back, routines are restored.

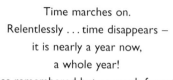

We don't yet see things clearly.
We're squinting in a fog, peering through a mist.
But it won't be long before the weather clears
and the sun shines bright!
We'll see it all then ...
as clearly as God sees us.
I Corinthians 13:12

There is a time for everything, and a season for
every activity under heaven:
a time to be born and a time to die ...
a time to weep and a time to laugh ...
a time to keep and a time to throw away ...
Ecclesiastes 3:1, 2, 4, 6

We owe it to ourselves
and to those we have loved and see no more
to rebuild life on the foundation
of love they have left us.
It is a way of showing our gratitude
to those who have tried to walk beside us
in our grieving
to pick up new threads and rejoin 'Life'.

As we are healing there will be others
just entering the long tunnel of despair.
We have been there – and so has God.
You are never alone.

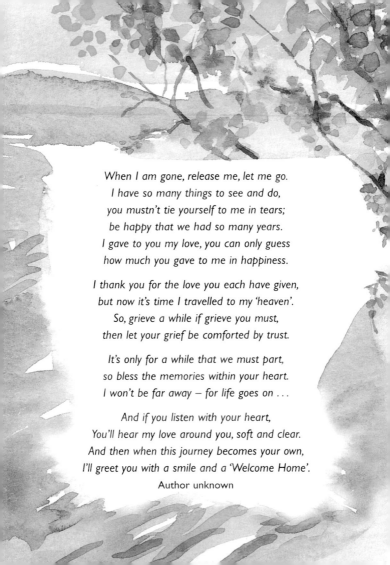

When I am gone, release me, let me go.
I have so many things to see and do,
you mustn't tie yourself to me in tears;
be happy that we had so many years.
I gave to you my love, you can only guess
how much you gave to me in happiness.

I thank you for the love you each have given,
but now it's time I travelled to my 'heaven'.
So, grieve a while if grieve you must,
then let your grief be comforted by trust.

It's only for a while that we must part,
so bless the memories within your heart.
I won't be far away – for life goes on . . .

And if you listen with your heart,
You'll hear my love around you, soft and clear.
And then when this journey becomes your own,
I'll greet you with a smile and a 'Welcome Home'.

Author unknown

Useful Addresses

SAMARITANS
The local number will be in the telephone book.

CRUSE
Cruse House, 126 Sheen Road, Richmond,
Surrey, TW9 1UR
0208 940 4818

COMPASSIONATE FRIENDS
6 Denmark Street, Bristol, BS1 5DQ
0272 539639

AGE CONCERN
Bernard Sunley House, 60 Pitcairn Road,
Mitcham, Surrey, CR4 3LL
0207 640 5431